Seneca Chief,
Army General

Seneca Chief, Army General

A Story about Ely Parker

by Elizabeth Van Steenwyk
illustrated by Karen Ritz

A Creative Minds Biography

M Millbrook Press/Minneapolis

*To Michael Jon, Aaron, and DK, whose paternal
great-great-grandmother was, like Ely Parker, a
citizen of two worlds*

A special word of thanks to William H. Armstrong. Without his careful research, this book could never have been written. Gratefully I acknowledge
the Huntington Library, San Marino, California, and its rare book section,
where I held Ely Parker's words in my hands.

Pronunciation note: The name Ely is pronounced EE-lee.

Text copyright © 2001 by Donald and Elizabeth Van Steenwyk Family Trust
Illustrations copyright © 2001 by Karen Ritz

This book is available in two editions:
Library binding by Millbrook Press,
    a division of Lerner Publishing Group, Inc.
Soft cover by LernerClassroom,
    an imprint of Lerner Publishing Group, Inc.
241 First Avenue North
Minneapolis, MN 55401 USA

For reading levels and more information, look up this title at
www.lernerbooks.com.

Library of Congress Cataloging-in-Publication Data

Van Steenwyk, Elizabeth.
    Seneca chief, army general : a story about Ely Parker / by Elizabeth
Van Steenwyk ; illustrated by Karen Ritz.
        p.   cm. — (A creative minds biography)
Includes bibliographical references and index.
Summary: Biography of the Seneca Indian who helped save his people's
land, was elected a sachem, served in the Union Army, became a general,
and was named commissioner of Indian affairs.
    ISBN 978-1-57505-431-5 (lib. bdg. : alk. paper)
    ISBN 978-1-57505-419-3 (pbk. : alk. paper)
    ISBN 978-1-57505-804-7 (eBook)
    1. Parker, Ely Samuel, 1828–1895—Juvenile literature. 2. Seneca
Indians—Biography—Juvenile literature. 3. Generals—United States—
Biography—Juvenile literature. 4. Indians of North America—
Government relations—Juvenile literature. [1. Parker, Ely Samuel,
1828–1895. 2. Seneca Indians. 3. Generals. 4. Indians of North
America—Government relations. 5. Indians of North America.] I. Ritz,
Karen, ill. II. Title. III. Series.
    E99.S3 P3257 2001
    974.7004'9755—dc21   99-050552

Manufactured in the United States of America
5 – DOC – 3/1/14

Table of Contents

1

The Broken Rainbow

Ten-year-old Ely Parker couldn't hold still. Sitting in church with his parents and listening to a preacher made him fidget. Besides, the preacher spoke English. When Ely chose to listen, he knew only a few words. He had attended a Baptist mission school for a while. There the lessons were taught in English. But when Ely returned to his parents' home, he forgot the little English he'd learned. He spoke only the soft sounds of his native Seneca, leaving the white man's language in the white man's school.

Ely longed to go outside and chase deer, go fishing, or race the wind. He looked around. Had anyone noticed how distracted he was? Many Seneca Indians were present on this day. The church was on their reservation, and many had adopted the Christian religion of their white neighbors. But they had not forgotten the ways of their ancestors.

Suddenly, one of the Seneca leaders stood up. The preacher, startled, stopped talking. Everyone watched as the Indian leader turned and pointed at Ely! The elder told the boy to translate. He wanted Ely to change the white man's words into their native tongue.

Ely stood up, walked slowly down the aisle, and faced the congregation. Maybe the elder thought Ely remembered English from school, but Ely hadn't paid attention to his lessons. He didn't know what to do. The preacher began to talk again, then waited for Ely to translate the words from English to Seneca.

Ely began to sweat. He felt his face turn dark with shame. His parents, his brothers and sister, his friends, and the elders waited for him to speak. But he couldn't. He couldn't say a word.

Ely Parker fainted.

Later, no one scolded him. No one laughed or made fun of him. His parents, William and Elizabeth Parker, understood that he was not yet ready for what had been asked of him. Elizabeth raised her children by the teachings of her great-grandfather Handsome Lake. He said that children learned by watching and listening to older people in their families. They learned nothing from harsh words or spankings.

Elizabeth Parker deeply loved all her children. But she knew that Ely's life would be different from the lives of his siblings. Four months before his birth, she had had a dream. She saw herself in the middle of a raging winter storm. Then the sky opened, and the clouds were swept back. Across the sky, Elizabeth saw a rainbow that was broken in the middle. It reached from the reservation to the Granger farm, the home of a white man who represented the United States government to the Indians.

When she awakened, Elizabeth had to know the meaning of her dream. So she went to ask the *djis-gadataha,* or dream teller, to explain the dream to her. He said that Elizabeth would have a son whose life would be divided like the rainbow. The boy would be born on the reservation and would be a peacemaker for his own people. But he would also live in the white man's world and take part in war. When he died, he would be buried on land that had once be-longed to his ancestors.

Four months later, in 1828, Elizabeth and William

Parker became the parents of a baby boy. The child never learned the exact date of his birth. His parents named him Hasanoanda, or "Leading Name." His father had taken the family's English last name, Parker, from a British officer who had been adopted by local Indians.

Elizabeth carried her new baby in a cradleboard on her back as she worked. She tended maple trees in the early spring, taking the children into the woods with her. There they boiled down sap to make syrup. Elizabeth also shot raccoons and rabbits and large birds to feed her growing family.

The Parkers lived in a two-story house on the Tonawanda Reservation in New York. The Seneca and the other five nations that belonged to the Iroquois Confederacy had once lived in a much larger area. Then, in the 1600s and 1700s, many Europeans came to live in North America. These new settlers claimed or bought most of the Iroquois land. By the 1800s, fewer than four thousand Indians lived on four small reservations. The Parkers and their relatives lived on one of them.

The lower floor of the Parkers' home had but one room, which was furnished with wooden benches. There the family ate, using dishes made of bark and wood. The Parkers loved to share their meals with company. They called out *"dadjoh,"* or "enter," to everyone who passed the house. Hasanoanda soon understood why people enjoyed coming to visit. Elizabeth was known all over the reservation for her fried bear and venison steaks. Always generous, she usually had a kettle of food warming over the fire.

People also came to listen to William Parker and his brothers talk about farming and milling. And the Seneca elders came to tell the fables they had learned from their ancestors. Everyone sat by the fire as the adults took turns speaking. One might tell of huge buffalo that tore down forests. Another would describe monster mosquitoes or giants made of stone.

The elders also shared their wisdom. They often repeated the teachings of Handsome Lake, Hasanoanda's great-great-grandfather. He believed that in order to live with their white neighbors, the Seneca must understand them. "So many white people are about you that you must study to know their ways," he had once said. Hasanoanda learned, too, about Red Jacket. Red Jacket was his mother's great-uncle. A famous speaker, he had received a medal from George Washington. It was a treasured gift.

Hasanoanda's imagination was stirred by what he heard, although his eyes grew heavy with sleep as the hour became late. Once in a while, the guests stayed all night. Then they rolled up in blankets and slept by the fire until morning, when Elizabeth began to pound corn for breakfast porridge.

As Hasanoanda grew, Elizabeth kept her dream and her great-grandfather's teachings in mind. She sent her son to the Baptist mission school to learn more of the ways of white people. He studied spelling, geography, and arithmetic. Only one thing stayed with him from the mission school—his new first name, Ely. A teacher, the Reverend Ely Stone, had given it to him. But most of Ely's book learning flew away like an eagle in the sky.

Ely's parents decided he needed more education after he left the mission school. When he was ten, they sent him to an Iroquois settlement on the Grand River in Ontario, Canada. There he learned more about outdoor life. Ely became skilled at using a gun, shooting a bow, handling a canoe, and crafting wood. He learned to track a deer over leaves and follow the trail of a snake.

In Canada, Ely grew tall and strong and became a teenager. But he felt more homesick each day. He missed his mother's cooking. He missed playing with his friends and younger brothers. And he missed the stories his relatives told around the fire. When Ely heard the Iroquois talk about his ancestors—Red

Jacket, Handsome Lake, and the Seneca leader Cornplanter—he longed to go home even more.

Finally, one day when Ely was about thirteen, he walked away from the Iroquois settlement. He didn't tell anyone he was leaving. He simply headed home, a distance of about one hundred miles. If he was afraid, he told no one that either. With his newfound knowledge of outdoor life, he began his trek through the forest. He traveled along streams and through meadows, heading east to the Tonawanda Reservation. His steps were swift and sure.

In Hamilton, Ontario, Ely met some British officers. (At that time, Canada was a British colony.) Hoping to make friends, he tried to talk with them in English. But he found he knew even fewer words than on that day in church. Yet he knew enough to understand that the British soldiers were making fun of him. They were telling jokes at his expense.

Ely Parker grew more determined as each step carried him closer to home. Never again would he be caught unable to speak or understand English. The white man's world was all about him, just as Handsome Lake had said long ago. Ely would enter it prepared.

2

A New World

Home again, Ely returned to the mission school. He studied hard until he felt ready to go on to a more advanced school. In the fall of 1842, he entered Yates Academy, twenty miles from home. The school was only a year old but already had two hundred students. Ely was the only Native American there, so he had to speak English all the time. "I feel myself crazy, in getting the two languages mixed into my head," he told his new classmates. But soon he could write English as well as speak it.

Ely joined a club called the Euglossian Society. The members liked to listen to speeches, and he liked to give them. He quickly became one of the club's favorites. When word got around on campus that Ely was speaking to the society, their meeting room overflowed with listeners.

At home on the reservation, the Seneca chiefs heard how easily Ely spoke the white people's tongue. Though he was only fourteen years old, they named him their interpreter. Ely began to write official papers for the Seneca. He also witnessed, or confirmed, the signature marks that the chiefs made on their letters to the United States government.

It was an important time for the Seneca, who were facing a terrible problem. They were going to lose their land. In 1838 some Seneca chiefs had signed a treaty. They agreed to sell their reservations to the Ogden Land Company and move to new homes in the western United States.

Later, the Seneca claimed that some of those chiefs had been elected illegally. Others had been bribed or confused by whiskey. In spite of these claims, the United States Senate voted to make the treaty a law. Unless something could be done, Ely and his friends and relatives would have to leave Tonawanda by April 1, 1846. They would be forced to resettle far away or become homeless.

In 1844 Ely went with elders from the reservation to Albany, the capital of New York. The elders wanted

Ely to tell the governor about the risk to the Seneca land. Ely worked with the elders for long hours, but he sometimes escaped the routine to visit stores in town. One day he was visiting his favorite bookstore. There he met a white man named Lewis Henry Morgan. Morgan was studying the lives of Indians in New York, so Ely invited him to meet the rest of the Seneca in Albany.

Ely's talk with the governor didn't help the Seneca, but his friendship with Lewis Henry Morgan grew. Morgan spoke with Ely and the elders each day, taking notes about their way of life. After Ely left Albany, he and Morgan wrote letters to each other. They began discussing Ely's education and future.

Ely's work as an interpreter took time away from his education. Still, his three years at Yates were some of the happiest of his life. He made several close friends and even began a romance with a white girl named Mary. Their friendship became the talk of the town.

Ely planned to take Mary for a buggy ride on the Fourth of July. When the day came, people filled the town's porches and stood on street corners. Everyone wanted to see if Mary's family would allow her to be seen in public with an Indian. Ely and Mary enjoyed their ride, but her parents quickly took her out of school. She did not return.

Soon after Ely finished at Yates in 1845, his friend Lewis Henry Morgan visited the Tonawanda Reservation. They went to a three-day meeting of the League of the Iroquois. More than five hundred Indians attended. New sachems, or league chiefs, were elected to lead the people through the struggle for the land. The elders made speeches. They reminded the people that Iroquois leaders of the past had predicted that those who sold land would be punished. The Indians became even more determined. They would not sell their land to anyone.

Ely thought he needed still more education, so Morgan helped him enter Cayuga Academy in Aurora, New York. At a time when few Native Americans were welcomed into white society, Ely was becoming more and more at home in this new world. But he was determined to maintain close ties with his people. He would enter Cayuga as a "son of the forest," he said. He would not forget his years on the reservation and in the Canadian wilderness.

Ely was pleased to learn that the academy occupied the hunting grounds of his ancestors. When he wasn't studying or going to class, he walked in the hills. He looked for arrows and charm stones, rocks that medicine men used to coax illness and bad spirits from a person's body.

Ely's studies presented no difficulties for him. But some of the students did. They resented him simply because he was an Indian. Some even picked fights with him. As Ely wrote in his diary, he "returned blow for blow." The fights were "bad business," he added, "but it could not be helped."

Ely had little time to pursue his studies in the next months, however. He became more involved in the struggle to save the Tonawanda Reservation. White settlers were already buying plots of reservation land, and something had to be done quickly to stop them. In January 1846, Ely traveled throughout New York. He asked people to sign petitions supporting the Seneca. He spoke to everyone who might be sympathetic to their cause.

The next month, Ely made his first trip to Washington, D.C. His mood was dark and angry. He hated the American capital, the home of the government that threatened his people. He wrote in his diary that he was afraid his race would soon "be lost to the memory of man."

Ely returned to Cayuga Academy. But within a month, the Seneca leaders called for his help again. They asked him to return to Washington. Ely realized he could not be a scholar and an interpreter at the same time. He left the academy for good. Filled with confidence, the eighteen-year-old prepared to go back to the capital. This time he was actually looking forward to the trip. He was going to meet the president of the United States!

3

Citizen of Two Worlds

Ely didn't have to wait long to meet President James K. Polk. After arriving with two Seneca chiefs on Monday, March 16, 1846, he spoke with the president the following Thursday. Ely found the American leader friendly and courteous. The meeting raised his hopes that the reservation would be saved. "Hurra for Polk!" he later wrote to a friend.

But the president had little time to think about Indian land troubles. He had something else on his mind—Texas. The United States and Mexico disagreed over the ownership of this huge territory. War was threatening. The president had to attend to the crisis immediately.

Six days passed before President Polk could see Ely and the Seneca chiefs again. Ely argued against the sale of the Tonawanda land. The president listened, then agreed to have the Senate look into the matter. Encouraged, the Seneca chiefs hired an attorney, William Linn Brown, to present their case to the senators. But Brown didn't represent the Seneca. Instead, he sailed to Cuba on a secret mission for President Polk.

By this time Ely had returned to New York to take up the cause there. When he heard about Brown's departure, he was furious and once again hurried back to Washington. There he met with the president alone. Ely reminded President Polk that the United States had signed a treaty of peace and friendship with the League of the Iroquois in 1794. He hoped the government would continue to honor it. President Polk was impressed. But he said that Congress needed time to review the treaties and decide how to proceed. Meanwhile, though, the Seneca would not be forced to leave their land. Ely had won a small victory.

Months went by, and Congress ended its session. The senators had made no decisions about the Seneca land dispute. Ely went home until it was time to argue the case again. On New Year's Day 1847, he returned to Washington. He felt so comfortable in the capital that he went alone to a large party at the White House. Ely was delighted when President Polk recognized him in the crowd.

The party was crowded and lively. Soon the rooms became so full that people couldn't exit through the doors. Instead, they climbed out of the windows. Before long, Ely climbed out of a window too. He moved on to another party at the home of Dolley Madison, the widow of former president James Madison. He was greeted politely there as well.

No one seemed offended by the presence of a Native American at the parties Ely attended on New Year's Day. But on Sunday it was a different story. When he entered a church, an usher abruptly told him he would have to sit upstairs. Ely left. In his diary he wrote that he would "rather be somewhere else" under such unwelcoming conditions.

As the weeks passed, Ely met with the senators one at a time. He presented his argument about the land treaty to each of them. Many were impressed by his ability to support his cause. But the Senate voted against the Indians and made the treaty a law. The Ogden Land Company would be allowed to force the Seneca from their reservations.

The Seneca didn't give up. They took their argument to the courts and began a series of lawsuits. But

Ely felt very discouraged by the Senate's decision. He was also deeply hurt to find himself criticized by his own people. They felt he had failed them. Some of the chiefs even accused him of plotting against the Seneca with the Ogden Land Company.

At home once again, Ely began to think about his future. Determined to make his way in the new world he had entered, he applied to Harvard College. He hoped to begin studying law. But no response came to his application. Then an offer arrived from a lawyer named William P. Angel. Angel suggested that Ely study in his office. In those days, men could study in a lawyer's office rather than attend school. If they studied hard enough to pass certain tests, they were allowed to become lawyers.

Ely accepted Angel's offer. Grateful to be free of the past year's responsibilities and criticism, he moved to Ellicottville, New York. His studies soon filled his time, but he went to parties whenever he could. And he joined an organization called the Masons. This group was devoted to building character through study and charity work. Ely loved the Masons' costumes and ceremonies. Best of all, they accepted him personally. In his Indian world, Ely belonged to the Seneca nation. In his white world, he belonged to the Masons.

In 1848 Ely's life was interrupted yet again by his people's needs. The Seneca elders had realized that no one could deal with white leaders as well as Ely could. They asked him to travel to Washington to check on their case. So Ely broke off his studies and left Ellicottville. As before, he was unable to help the Seneca. But the trip left him with a wonderful memory that he cherished all his life.

As Ely walked down the street one day, the president's wife, Sarah Polk, stopped her carriage. She asked if she could take Ely to his destination. Ely was thrilled to ride through the streets of Washington with the First Lady. It was another sign of his growing acceptance in the new world he was exploring, the world of white America.

Ely stopped his studies to help with reservation problems many times. But he continued to learn about the law. He also wrote long essays about Iroquois traditions. Ely gave many of his essays to Lewis Henry Morgan, who was writing a book about the Iroquois. No one had ever made a written record of many of the traditions Ely described. Without his work, this knowledge might have been lost forever.

In late 1848, Ely finally felt ready to pass the law exam. Then he learned of another obstacle in his path. Only citizens of the United States could become lawyers. According to the law, Indians were not citizens. Even after all of Ely's preparation, he could not practice law. His acceptance in the capital had been as an intelligent young Indian leader, not as an American citizen.

Fortunately, Ely was tough enough not to let this disappointment discourage him for long. By the end of the year, he was looking for another career, eager to move on with life in both of his worlds.

4

A New Direction

Ely turned to his friend Lewis Henry Morgan for help. Morgan suggested civil engineering—the planning and building of roads, bridges, and buildings. Morgan knew that engineering jobs could be found in New York. Such a job would keep Ely in the state. Morgan still needed Ely's help with his book about the League of the Iroquois.

Ely took his friend's advice. Early in 1849, he moved to Nunda, New York, and began to work on the Genesee Valley Canal. He chopped down trees with an axe while the other men in the crew surveyed, or measured, the land. Ely learned this new profession quickly. He also continued to learn the social skills of his white neighbors—even country dancing.

Although Ely was more comfortable than ever in white society, he never forgot the skills he had learned as a Seneca boy. One night he attended a dance in a village near Nunda, then spent the night there at a hotel. The next morning, he saw deer tracks outside.

Ely followed the tracks and caught up with the deer. Then he killed it and carried it over his shoulder back to the hotel. His wilderness training hadn't left him.

Ely liked his job, but he was restless. He moved on to another job in Rochester, New York. He thought more and more about moving to the West. Perhaps his future would be brighter there. Meanwhile, Lewis Henry Morgan's book about the Iroquois was published in 1851. It became an important work in a new field—anthropology, the study of the origins and customs of human beings. Morgan dedicated the book to Ely, thanking him for his help with the research.

Ely's life took a new turn that September. At the age of twenty-three, he was elected one of fifty new sachems of the League of the Iroquois. The entire league had recognized his talents and loyalty at last. As a sachem, Ely wasn't put in charge of making laws or ruling his people. He was recognized as one of many leaders among the Iroquois, one whose views would be respected. He also received a new name, Donehogawa, or "Open Door."

Impressed with Ely's leadership, the Iroquois council honored him in another way. They presented him with the medal that George Washington had given to Ely's ancestor, Red Jacket, in 1792. Ely wore this badge of respect proudly at Iroquois functions.

31

As a sachem, Ely continued to travel to Washington on behalf of the Seneca. He also kept working in Rochester. He enjoyed living there, but soon he was ready to move on. In 1857 he got his chance. The government gave him the position he'd been waiting for out west. He would become a civil engineer in Galena, Illinois.

Some people in Galena didn't like the idea of an Indian holding a government post. But Ely arrived in April to build a hospital and a customhouse, a building where taxes would be collected from boats on the Galena River. The job was demanding. Every decision he made had to be approved by officials in Washington. Ely learned to be patient. While he waited, he tried to make new friends. But social life in the West wasn't quite what Ely had expected. He missed the elegant parties of New York and Washington, where he had always been welcome.

Three months after Ely came to Galena, the Seneca called on him for help again. So he traveled to Washington to meet with President James Buchanan and his staff. Together they solved the land problems at long last. The Seneca agreed to pay the Ogden Land Company for most of the land. Ely's family and friends were secure. They could keep their Tonawanda homes forever.

Ely Parker had spent fourteen years helping the Seneca save their land. At last he could focus on his life and work in Galena. Sadly, many people did not welcome him. Indians and white pioneers had fought openly in Illinois as recently as the 1830s. Many citizens remembered those days. Even though Ely was a Seneca from New York, they didn't want a successful Indian in their town.

Fortunately for Ely, Galena had a chapter of the Masons. There he found acceptance and many friendships. He began to like his new home better. In fact, when he returned to Tonawanda for a visit, he was surprised to find himself homesick for Illinois.

In 1860 Ely met a former army officer named Ulysses S. Grant. Grant was a quiet man. He showed his warmer side only after he settled into a new friendship. As Ely said many years later, "[Grant] reminded me of some of my Indian friends. It was necessary to break the ice before the good qualities of the [man] could be seen."

A barroom brawl helped forge their friendship. One day, as Ely walked past a tavern, he heard Grant's voice among those of many angry men. Ely stepped in and found his friend fighting a roomful of opponents. Ely stood back-to-back with Grant as they fended off attackers with their fists. The two men learned an important lesson that day. They could depend on each other in a crisis.

That fall an election took place. As an Indian, Ely wasn't allowed to vote, but he supported Stephen Douglas for president. Douglas was defeated by Abraham Lincoln. Because Ely worked for the government, some politicians demanded that he be replaced. They argued that his position should go to someone who had not opposed the new president. Ely lost his job in March 1861.

Lincoln's election affected the entire country. For years Americans had disagreed about slavery. Laws in the South allowed people to buy and sell African Americans as slaves, while in the North slavery was illegal. Lincoln believed that slavery should end. After he became president, many Southern states left the United States. Lincoln and Congress decided to try to hold the nation together. They failed, and the Civil War began in April 1861.

Both Ely and his friend Ulysses S. Grant supported the North. Grant decided to seek an appointment as an officer in the Northern army. He urged Ely to join the army as well. So Ely went home to the Tonawanda Reservation. He would find out if he had a place in this country's war—despite the fact that he was not even considered an American citizen.

5

The White Man's War

Ely didn't stay at Tonawanda for long. He traveled to Washington to offer his services to the War Department. He spoke with William H. Seward, the secretary of state. Ely thought that Seward would understand why he wanted to enter the North's Union army. But Seward wasted no words in dismissing him. The war must be settled by white men, Seward said. "Go home [and] cultivate your farm," he added. "We will settle our own troubles among ourselves without any Indian aid."

Those were harsh words for Ely to hear, but he did go home. "[I] planted crops and myself" at Tonawanda, he wrote. Seward's words didn't discourage him. He grew even more determined to find his place in this conflict between the North and the South. Ely remembered how his lack of citizenship had kept him from becoming a lawyer. So he asked Congress to make him a citizen. But this request was turned down, too.

Finally, Ely resigned himself to life on his people's reservation. He farmed his family's acres but found little satisfaction in the work. Depressed, he wrote to a friend, "I am stuck, and must remain so until I can get out."

Then Elizabeth Parker became ill. She died on the morning of February 23, 1862. Ely and his brother Levi traveled to the town of Akron to buy a coffin for their mother. Another brother, Newton, prepared Elizabeth for burial in the Seneca way. He clothed her in a red dress, black beaded leggings, deerskin moccasins, and a traditional cape. Her funeral took place on a stormy day. "This [death] throws a great gloom upon our family," Ely wrote.

After Elizabeth's funeral, Ely tried again to enter the army. He had been at Tonawanda for almost two years when he received an unexpected letter. He had been made a captain! The appointment came from John E. Smith, an old friend from the Galena Masons. Smith had become a brigadier general in the Union army. His commander was another old friend of Ely's, Ulysses S. Grant.

Ely was told to report for duty in Vicksburg, Mississippi. But before he left, he had to say good-bye to his friends and relatives. Six hundred of them gathered on the Tonawanda Reservation in June 1863.

In a moving ceremony, the Seneca council gave over Ely's care and well-being to the Great Spirit. They also granted Ely permission to serve the United States government in its war. After Ely received the council's blessing, he left for Vicksburg. His beloved Red Jacket medal journeyed with him.

Thirty-five-year-old Ely Parker looked handsome in the blue uniform of the Union army. He stood five feet, eight inches tall. A friend said that he weighed "two hundred pounds of encyclopedia," referring to his intelligence as well as his size. He spoke English without an accent in a deep voice, and his erect posture gave him a military air. He could defend himself physically when he needed to, yet he never looked for a fight. He was even known for his gentleness.

Ely arrived at General Smith's headquarters in July, just after the South's Confederate army had given up the city of Vicksburg to the North. For a few months, Ely served as an engineer. In September he was transferred to General Grant's personal staff. Grant needed an officer to help write out and distribute his orders, and Ely's legal skills and talent with words made him the perfect choice.

Shortly after his transfer, Ely became sick with a terrible fever. He probably had a disease called malaria. Because malaria is carried by mosquitoes, it can spread quickly. It had killed many men during the battle for Vicksburg. (During the Civil War, disease killed more soldiers than bullets did.) Fortunately, Ely recovered. But he lost thirty pounds and was weak for days afterward.

As Ely began to grow stronger, a new battle shaped up near Chattanooga, Tennessee. This time he got a firsthand glimpse of the war. As a member of the general's staff, Ely wasn't a soldier in the usual sense. He didn't actually take part in the fighting. But since he was at the general's side most of the time, he got a close-up view of the battle and came under fire often. In his letters home, Ely claimed that the noise and bullets didn't bother him. "No more danger is paid to [the Confederates'] firing than to a boy playing with a pop gun," he wrote.

To Ely, the battle of Chattanooga was "a splendid affair." General Grant, puffing on a cigar, watched the battle with Ely from Orchard Knob. The Union troops fired on the Confederates, who had dug in on Missionary Ridge. The response was deafening. Smoke billowed over the battlefield. Under constant fire, the Union soldiers drove their opponents back and took Lookout Mountain. After three long days of fighting, the battle ended in victory for the North.

Ely's admiration of General Grant grew throughout

the battle. Danger didn't seem to bother him. He was often on the front lines, near the worst of the fighting. He never seemed to notice the bullets and shells whizzing nearby. Grant didn't bother using roads to travel, either. He preferred to take shortcuts through fields and woods. Often he rode from breakfast until late at night without stopping to eat.

Ely wasn't the only person who admired Ulysses S. Grant's leadership in battle. President Lincoln made Grant commander of all the Northern armies in March 1864. Grant chose Ely and a few other staff members to go with him to Washington, D.C., to take charge.

Ely took several days off to visit the reservation before going to Grant's new headquarters. Ely's father was sick and wasn't expected to live, so the few hours Ely spent with him meant a great deal. William Parker died in April. With both his parents dead, Ely said he was "afloat and without an anchor in this wide world." His link to the reservation weakened.

But the war continued, and Ely turned his full attention to duty. General Grant made preparations to capture Richmond, Virginia, the Confederate capital. On May 7, the general moved his headquarters closer to the battlefield. But the nearby woods were on fire, and men and wagons blocked the roads. So Grant and his men turned off onto a dark side road. Ely recalled his childhood training in how to find his way through wilderness. He realized that Grant was heading directly into the enemy camp.

Ely asked General Grant if he knew where he was. He didn't. Ely immediately turned his horse and led the group to safety. After the war, he spoke to a former Confederate general about that night. He learned that a group of Confederates had seen Grant and his party riding along that side road. They were waiting to take them by surprise when the Northern soldiers suddenly turned away. The Confederates had always wondered what caused the Northerners to reverse their direction.

Danger awaited Ely everywhere. One time he was riding down a country road with John Rawlins, another member of Grant's staff. Suddenly, Confederate guns fired directly at them. Ely saw a cannonball coming and ducked. The ball grazed his sleeve as it went by. Later, he wrote to a friend, "This life, though dangerous, suits me charmingly."

Most of the time, Ely's presence and work on General Grant's staff were accepted by all who met him. But a few of the officers disliked him—just as they disliked all Indians. Some even looked for ways to hurt his reputation. One officer, Harry Wilson, claimed he had seen Ely drunk on the battlefield.

He wrote that Ely, "like all Indians, [was] accustomed to getting drunk occasionally." It is true that Ely sometimes drank alcohol, just as many white officers did. But many people were too willing to believe that an Indian drank too much—even without proof.

General Grant, however, liked Ely and found his work excellent. In August 1864, he asked Ely to become his military secretary. With the promotion, Ely became a lieutenant colonel. He no longer just wrote copies of orders; he helped the general write letters, too. These new duties brought him closer than ever to Grant. He spent much of his time at the general's side, writing messages. Ely carried Grant's official papers in a folder and wore a wooden bottle of ink tied to his buttonhole with a leather cord.

The secretary and the general were alike in many ways. They both enjoyed a good cigar and a stroll after their evening meal. Neither talked a lot, and both wrote down their thoughts more often than they spoke them. Each seemed to know how the other would act in a situation. Over time, a feeling of trust developed between them.

As the November election neared in 1864, many soldiers were granted leave to go home to vote. The law didn't allow Ely to vote, but he went home, too. He heard about the activities of other Seneca serving in the army, especially his brother Newton. And he heard about his sister Caroline's romance with a chief of the Tuscarora Indians. When Caroline moved to her new husband's farm, one more tie to home was broken for Ely. Meanwhile, the country's voters reelected Abraham Lincoln.

When Ely returned to headquarters in City Point, Virginia, he saw that log huts had replaced the summer tents. Grant's army would spend the winter there. The camp was close to Washington, so many government officials visited. One was William H. Seward, the secretary of state. No one knows whether he recognized Ely as the Indian he'd told to go home and stay out of the white man's war.

President Lincoln visited the camp, too. He stayed for more than two weeks. Ely talked with him many times, especially about the rights of Indians. Lincoln said he hoped the nation would one day right the wrongs it had inflicted on the Indians.

In spring the army moved into action again. Grant's men captured Richmond on April 2. The victory sent General Robert E. Lee and his Confederate troops south in one last effort to escape. But Lee's soldiers were worn out and starving. On April 9, Lee agreed to meet Grant in the village of Appomattox Court House to surrender.

Ely went with the general to the house where the meeting was to take place. Lee arrived in his best uniform, Grant in his wrinkled and muddy field uniform. At first Ely and the rest of the staff sat on the porch. But then General Grant invited them inside to meet the Confederate general. Lee shook hands with each soldier but said nothing. When Ely came before him, however, Lee paused to look at him for several seconds. Then he shook his hand and said, "I am glad to see one real American here."

"We are all Americans," Ely replied.

The generals spoke politely for a few minutes. Then Grant asked for an order book in which to write the terms of surrender. Ely added a few changes until both generals were satisfied. Then, as a personal honor to another member of his staff, Grant asked Theodore Bowers to write the final version of the peace agreement. Nervous, Bowers tried to write it three or four times. Finally, he turned the book over to Ely. "Parker, you will have to write this," Bowers said. "I can't do it."

So Ely Parker wrote the peace agreement that ended the Civil War. A few Confederate generals hadn't yet surrendered. But the war's outcome was certain at last. Ely kept a copy of the agreement as a souvenir of that historic day.

The next morning, the generals rode out to a point overlooking the Confederate camp. The other officers circled them on their horses, out of hearing. Only Ely stayed by Grant's side. Using an old tree stump as a desk, he wrote out a few more terms of surrender as the two generals talked.

Later that afternoon, General Lee turned his gray horse, Traveler, south for his homeward journey. General Grant and his staff began their trip back to Washington to meet with President Lincoln. A few days later, Ely met privately with the president and his family. He showed them his Red Jacket medal, the symbol of respect and peace between his people and the American government.

It was the last time Ely would ever see Abraham Lincoln. That night, as Ely traveled back to New York on leave, Lincoln and his wife went to a play. There Lincoln was shot by John Wilkes Booth. Booth was a Southerner who blamed the president for the Confederate defeat. Lincoln died early the next morning, April 15, 1865. A nation that was weary of sorrow was thrown into mourning once again.

6

An Indian General

Even as the nation mourned Abraham Lincoln, General Grant became the hero of the hour. Crowds surged around him wherever he went. He had to be protected by members of his staff. Ely wondered how the nation could celebrate the end of the war when President Lincoln had just been murdered. He remarked, "I am of a race which never forgives the murder of a friend."

The war was over, but the army still needed Ely. In July 1865, he met with a group of Indians from the southwestern United States. Slave owners themselves, some had fought against the North during the war. Ely helped work out a peace agreement between the government and these Indians.

General Grant recognized Ely's work by making him a brigadier general in 1866. More and more, Grant depended on Ely's advice about how to handle the army's many problems with Indians. Soon Grant asked him to submit a plan for dealing with Indians in the West, where the problems were the worst.

Many white settlers had moved to the West throughout the 1800s. The western Indians were being crowded from their homes onto reservations. The government paid agents to sell supplies on the reservations, but many agents were dishonest. They charged high prices for poor goods. But the Indians had to buy them because they had no other place to go. These difficult conditions had led to violence in many parts of the West.

In January 1867, Ely finished his plan. He suggested that the army take control over Indian affairs. The army could replace the dishonest agents with honest officers, Ely wrote. He added that all the Indians should be guaranteed territories of their own.

White settlers should not be allowed to live on this land. Congress did not adopt Ely's plan, but it proved an important point. Here in Washington lived and worked an Indian general whose voice spoke with strength and compassion. It was a voice that deserved to be heard.

Later that year, Ely met a young woman named Minnie Orton Sackett. She was beautiful, talkative, and lively. Within months they announced their engagement and became the talk of the capital. He was a thirty-nine-year-old Seneca chief. She was an eighteen-year-old member of white society. The wedding was scheduled for December 17 at a Washington church. General Grant came, planning to give the bride away. The church filled with friends and relatives, but at the appointed hour, the groom didn't appear. He seemed to have vanished.

Stories flew around Washington about Ely's disappearance. Some said that he had been drugged by another Indian to prevent him from marrying a white woman. Many Indians, including Handsome Lake, Ely's great-great-grandfather, viewed marriage between the two races as a sin.

No one ever knew for certain where Ely was. But on his return a few days later, his explanation must have satisfied Minnie. The wedding was rescheduled.

On December 24, three thousand curious people showed up to see if Ely would appear. The guests were disappointed to learn that the bride and groom, eager to avoid a scene, had married and left for their honeymoon the night before. They soon settled into married life in Washington.

Just as Ely's personal life was changing, his work changed, too. General Grant was elected president in November 1868. Soon after, he made Ely commissioner of Indian affairs. Ely would supervise the government's relationship with the nation's Indians. President Grant expected him to aid in the "civilization and . . . citizenship" of "the original occupants of the land."

This idea of "civilizing" the Indians weighed on Ely's mind. Many white Americans believed that the Indians should give up their languages and customs for the ways of white people. Ely knew that if this continued to happen, much of Indian culture would disappear forever. But he believed that Indians could no longer live as they once had. They would have to adjust to their white neighbors in order to survive. His job was to help them do so.

Grant also wanted the Indians to become United States citizens. This subject concerned Ely personally. To become commissioner of Indian affairs, he would have to be an American citizen. In 1866 Congress had granted citizenship to all American-born men. But this law excluded "Indians not taxed." Indians who lived on reservations generally didn't pay taxes to the government. So Indian men weren't considered citizens. Ely didn't live on a reservation anymore, though. And he worked for the government and the army. Was he a citizen? President Grant took the question to the attorney general, Ebenezer Hoar. He ruled that Ely was indeed a citizen and could serve as commissioner.

Ely found his new work fascinating. Indians from all over the country called on him in his office. Some dressed in traditional clothes with tomahawks at their belts. They sat on the floor because they weren't used to sitting on chairs. Ely listened to their concerns both as an Indian and as a representative of the government. He and his visitors often smoked a sacred peace pipe as they spoke.

Ely felt determined to do well at another important part of his job. He wanted to make sure the Indians received the goods the government promised to them. Before he took office, Ely had heard that goods had been stolen before they even reached the Indians. How could Indians settle on their reservations and become farmers without good tools and warm clothes?

Although more than six hundred employees reported to him, he personally checked the purchase and packing of as many boxes of clothing, bedding, and tools as he could.

President Grant set up the Board of Indian Commissioners to help Ely prevent theft. Ely was pleased more people would be helping the Indians. But soon after he took office, a commissioner asked to inspect a batch of goods that Ely had already checked. These goods had to reach the reservations quickly. Ely sent the shipment on rather than slow it down for another inspection. The commissioner found this behavior strange. He wondered if Ely was covering up a crime.

Ely tried to ignore the board's suspicion and simply do his job. He was concerned about getting promised food, clothing, and shelter to several groups of western Indians. In exchange, the Indians had agreed to remain at peace on their reservations. But the money to buy goods for the Indians was running out. Congress had only approved enough to last until July 1, 1870. The government's supplier would not send anything to the Indians beyond that date.

The western Indians might starve without the promised food. They might die without warm clothing and shelter. In their despair they might even start a war with nearby settlers. Ely found another supplier. This man agreed to ship emergency goods and accept payment later, after Congress approved it. In this way Ely kept his word and helped the western Indians. He probably prevented a war with them as well. Finally, on July 15, Congress passed a bill to provide additional supplies.

When Ely returned from a trip west in 1871, he was shocked. He had been accused of mishandling the purchase of the emergency supplies! Ely's accuser was William Welsh, a former member of the Board of Indian Commissioners. Welsh said Ely should have talked to the board about the purchase. Welsh also said Ely had paid too much for poor-quality goods. He even suggested Ely had taken a bribe to buy the emergency supplies. Welsh had no evidence to back up his claims. But a committee of the House of Representatives began to investigate Ely's honesty.

Ely appeared before the committee to defend himself. Although he seemed calm and confident, he felt deeply hurt. He had served the United States government faithfully for years. Was this his reward? Ely told the representatives, "I have never sought to defraud the Government of one penny, or have knowingly lent my aid to others with that view."

Soon the investigation ended. The committee

found that the only poor-quality goods Ely had sent west were a few blankets in the wrong color! Ely's attorney also showed that he had not acted wrongly under the law. He was allowed to make emergency purchases without the board's approval. As some people began to suspect, Ely's only "crime" was being an Indian.

The House committee reported that Ely had committed no crime. But they also said he should have asked President Grant to approve his emergency purchases. Congress made a new law. Ely would have to ask the Board of Indian Commissioners to approve all purchases—even the everyday ones.

Ely realized this law would slow down every action in his office. With so little power, he would hardly be able to help the Indians at all. So he resigned in August 1871. Although President Grant supported Ely and believed in his honesty, he accepted the resignation.

Sadly, Ely ended his ties to the government he had served for years. He and Minnie moved to Fairfield, Connecticut. They bought a house and settled down. Eventually, Ely went to work as a clerk in the New York City police department. His job had little responsibility. But in his usual way, he did it well and without complaint.

Ely's life brightened in 1878. At the age of fifty, he became a father. He and Minnie named their daughter Maud. Ely also gave the child a Seneca name, Ahweheeyo, or "Beautiful Flower." His family kept him busy, but he belonged to many veterans' organizations as well. Whenever he could, he saw his close friends from General Grant's staff. When Grant died in 1885, Ely and his comrades marched together in the funeral procession.

Once in a while, Ely returned to the reservation. He was glad to hear and speak his native Seneca. He said that he "went back home to loosen up my tongue." But Ely never returned permanently, since his ties to the reservation were no longer close. He knew that Minnie and Maud would never feel at home there. He would live out the rest of his days in the second of his two worlds.

In 1890 Ely became ill with diabetes. He continued to work as long as he could. When several strokes weakened him, he was forced to retire. He died on August 30, 1895, at the age of sixty-seven.

Representatives from the two worlds of Ely Parker gathered for his funeral. On his casket lay one floral arrangement in the shape of the Christian cross and another in the shape of a door. The door symbolized Ely's role as the Seneca sachem called Donehogawa, or "Open Door." He was eventually buried in Forest Lawn Cemetery in Buffalo, New York, near a statue of his ancestor Red Jacket. The cemetery was located on the old Granger farm where the Iroquois Indians once had traded.

And so the prophecy of the dream teller came true. Long ago Elizabeth Parker, Ely's mother, had asked her people's dream teller, the *djisgadataha,* to tell her the meaning of the broken rainbow in her dream. She learned that she would have a son and that "his sun will rise on Indian land and set on the white man's land. Yet the ancient land of his ancestors will fold him in death."

The ancient land held him at last.

60

Bibliography

Armstrong, William H. *Warrior in Two Camps: Ely S. Parker, Union General and Seneca Chief.* Syracuse, NY: Syracuse University Press, 1978.

Bruchac, Joseph. "The White Man's War: Ely Parker: Iroquois General." *Northeast Indian Quarterly* (fall 1988): 40–48.

Hauptmann, Laurence M. "Iroquois in Blue: From Reservation to Civil War Battlefield." *Northeast Indian Quarterly* (fall 1988): 35–40.

Knight, Margaret, and Karen Bordner Brechner. "The Mystery of Ely Parker." *Rensselaer: The Alumni Magazine* (June 1991): 24–30.

Liberty, Margot, ed. *American Indian Intellectuals.* St. Paul, MN: West Publishing Company, 1978.

McFeely, William S. *Grant.* New York: W. W. Norton and Company, 1981.

Parker, Arthur C. *The Life of General Ely S. Parker, Last Grand Sachem of the Iroquois and General Grant's Military Secretary.* Buffalo, NY: Buffalo Historical Society, 1919.

Parker, Ely S. Papers. Henry E. Huntington Library, San Marino, CA.

Snow, Dean R. *The Iroquois.* Cambridge, MA: Blackwell, 1994.

Index

About the Author

Elizabeth Van Steenwyk loves to share unusual stories with young readers. She has written about the California gold rush, medicine on the American frontier, and the lives of fascinating people such as Civil War photographer Mathew Brady and artist Frederic Remington, as well as the characters in her many works of fiction. Ms. Van Steenwyk decided to write about Ely Parker because she felt that children deserved to learn about the accomplishments of this amazing Native American. She lives in California, where she divides her time between her home in San Marino and her family's ranch and winery in Paso Robles.

About the Illustrator

Karen Ritz has been practicing drawing since she was a child living in upstate New York. She later moved to Minnesota and earned a degree in children's literature from the University of Minnesota. Since then, she has combined two of her favorite pastimes, reading and drawing, by becoming a children's book illustrator. Ms. Ritz lives in St. Paul with her husband and three children. She has illustrated many books, including several for Carolrhoda Books.